Textures

Textures

John Eppel
and
Togara Muzanenhamo

with an introduction by Drew Shaw

'amaBooks

ISBN 978-0-7974-9498-5
EAN 9780797494985

Published by 'amaBooks
P.O. Box AC1066, Ascot, Bulawayo
amabooksbyo@gmail.com
www.amabooksbyo.com

Cover Design: Veena Bhana

Cover Art: Helen Lieros

Togara Muzanenhamo would like to express his gratitude to Lancaster Park and The Rockefeller Foundation for their support.

'All the Good Help' first appeared in *Granta*, 'Dorothy Recollects' in *New Coin*, 'Engine Philosophers' in *KIN*, 'Hornbills in My Garden' in *Carapace*, 'Mercantile Rain' in *Almost Island*, 'Peruvian Sunsets' in *Shoes or No Shoes*, 'Religion' in *Eleven Eleven*, and 'Savannah Chapel' and 'Zvita' in *Gumiguru*, Carcanet Press (2014).

Contents

About the authors

John Eppel, born in 1947, is an English teacher in Bulawayo. He published his first poems in the 1960s, in *Two Tone*, and his first collection, *Spoils of War*, in 1989. John won the Ingrid Jonker Prize for Poetry for *Spoils of War*, and the M-Net prize for his first novel, *D G G Berry's The Great North Road*. His second novel, *Hatchings*, was chosen for the series in the *Times Literary Supplement* of the most significant books to have come out of Africa. His other novels are *The Giraffe Man*, *The Curse of the Ripe Tomato*, *The Holy Innocents*, *Absent: The English Teacher*, *Traffickings* and *The Boy Who Loved Camping*.
John's other poetry collections are *Sonata for Matabeleland*, *Selected Poems: 1965-1995* and *Songs My Country Taught Me*. Two collections of his poetry and short stories have been published: *The Caruso of Colleen Bawn* and *White Man Crawling*.
Poems and short stories of Eppel's have appeared online and in many anthologies and journals, and his recent collaborations with other writers include *Together*, with Julius Chingono, and *Hewn from the Rock*, with Philani A Nyoni.

Born in 1975, Togara Muzanenhamo studied Business Administration in the Netherlands and in France. He has worked as a journalist and a film script editor. His poems have appeared widely in international magazines, journals and anthologies. In 2006 his debut collection of poems, *Spirit Brides*, was published by Carcanet Press and shortlisted for the Jerwood Aldeburgh First Collection Prize. The *Times Literary Supplement* welcomed the poet as a young writer of solid distinction: '*he can be "cool" but seldom "light". His best writing makes no reference to itself, does not allow itself to be damaged by over exuberant metaphor.*' In 2012 Muzanenhamo was chosen to represent Zimbabwe at Poetry Parnassus in London, 'the biggest gathering of poets in world history', where he read at the gala event with Seamus Heaney, Kim Hyesoon, Bill Manhire, Kay Ryan and Wole Soyinka at the Royal Festival Hall. Poetry Parnassus was part of the Cultural Olympiad that preceded the 2012 Olympic Games. His second collection, *Gumiguru*, is published by Carcanet Press.

Introduction

Dr Drew Shaw, 2014

In Zimbabwe, John Eppel and Togara Muzanenhamo epitomise the ideal of the poet dedicated to excellence in form as well as content. There are as many definitions of poetry as there are poets but, as the Merriam-Webster Dictionary usefully explains, poetry is "Writing that formulates a concentrated imaginative awareness of experience in language chosen and arranged to create a specific emotional response through its meaning, sound, and rhythm...." Poetry distinguishes itself from prose, moreover, by "compression, frequent use of conventions of metre and rhyme, [and] use of the line as a formal unit...." In their arrangement of words and creation of sounds and rhythms, John Eppel and Togara Muzanenhamo promote this classic view of poetry. I was fortunate to talk to both about this remarkable collaboration and it is a pleasure to introduce a very fine anthology.

To read *Textures* is to see how Eppel and Muzanenhamo are in many ways similar yet also interestingly different. What connects them is meticulous attention to the craft of poetry, particularly to its musical elements. As Eppel explained, "there's this kind of paradox with lyric poets where they actually want to get rid of words, but the only way they can get rid of words is by using words. So there's this movement away from sense dominating to sound dominating."

Both poets considered musical metaphors for the title of this collection but eventually chose the more visual name *Textures*, which is appropriate, Eppel said, "because the word 'text' is from the Latin *texere*, which basically means to weave, hence the word *textile*. So texture relates to the quality of woven cloth – and the idea of woof and the warp is appropriate for two poets who are interweaving their texts in one book." Muzanenhamo added: "Weaving is also a precise craft, which links what we're doing - which is weaving words, making some sort of music." One can imagine the rattle of a loom creating these poetic textures.

On commonalities, Muzanenhamo said, "I think, fundamentally, we're similar because we're adhering to a core structure of poetry – the rhythm, rhyme... the classics. In John's poetry, you can see classical forms like villanelles, sonnets, terza rima, sestinas, odes... I have explored these structures and will sometimes intentionally distort their frames to allow some sort of modern usage. But I'm still very much aware of where they came from, and where the structure is." To this Eppel added, "Togara is somebody who knows the 'rules', and so he can break them in ways that suit his intentions, whereas I stick to the rules deliberately, and part of this, of course, is a way of self-mockery. I give myself very rigid forms. I count the syllables. I work out the rhyme schemes very carefully. And then, within that frame, I do a little bit of twisting and distorting. I free myself a little bit within that trap. Whereas Togara frees himself beyond that. He will take control of a structure and adjust it, break it. So you can read some of his poems and you can see a sonnet there, but on top of that is another text; it becomes a palimpsest. You can do that well only if you know the basic rules."

Eppel's poems in this collection are mostly set in his hometown of Bulawayo and, in his own words, are "very rooted here in Matabeleland". This is one of the most noticeable differences between him and the more international Muzanenhamo. It used to be frowned upon in southern African literary circles, Eppel explained, to write outside the local context. For a new generation, however, this has changed dramatically, not least because of mass migration, globalisation and increased international travel.

Being of an older generation, Eppel still acknowledges what DH Lawrence calls "the spirit of place", which Eppel explores close to home. His own back garden is often the setting for his nature studies, and there is, for example, a sonnet sequence about Hillside Dams, a popular conservancy in Bulawayo's eastern suburbs, where Eppel walks with his dogs. With this sequence Eppel said he was responding – at least partly – to David Hughes, author of *Whiteness in Zimbabwe* (2010), who accuses white writers, including Eppel, of appropriating African landscapes, fetishising nature and imposing Europeanised aesthetics as a means of escape. Hughes apparently did not recognise that Eppel has spent a lifetime satirising this practice. [See Wylie (2012: 189-190).]

Eppel's 'Appropriating the Land' repeats a past project, which is to send up the colonial exercise: "We did dams... We erected bossy warnings... We wrote poems about sunsets/ jacarandas, blue skies...." 'Aloes at Hillside Dams' also unsettles the idea of taming nature to promote a particular ordering or indulge an escapism: here the pointed, clawed aloes, personified and with minds of their own, are unruly: "...in their multitudes/ they elaborate these Dams... /... as comrades, citizens, darlings, dudes." With Eppel, landscapes – even supposedly colonial landscapes such as the Hillside Dams conservancy – ruffle rather than maintain certainties and hence present a challenge to Hughes's oversimplified analysis. On another level, one of the Hillside Dam sonnets, 'Looking for You', deals movingly with love, loss and loneliness.

I went on to ask Eppel why birds are especially prominent in this collection. "I'm not sure why that's happened," he reflected. "Of course birds are an archetypal symbol of life, of a link to the metaphysical – consider the soapstone birds of Great Zimbabwe – and maybe that's what I'm clinging to, that sense of the spontaneous life in the bird as it flies up into the infinite." Also, he admitted, "I've always been a bit obsessed with flowers... and not just because they are pretty things with erotic connotations. I also use flowers to make fun of myself as a colonial, because the idea of planting pretty flowers instead of using the land to feed yourself is a very colonial thing."

Unmissable in this collection is Eppel's reflection on the passage of time, for example in 'Beauty is Truth, Truth Death'. Seasonal change, twilight and ageing set the mood for many of the poems and, like Thomas Hardy (the poet he most admires), Eppel now seems particularly poignant in later life. The voice of a recognisably older speaker comments on the cycle of life and death. On ageing Eppel said, "I don't think perspectives change much. It's just that as you get older you have a much more powerful sense of mortality; so you don't take being alive for granted anymore. But you don't see life and death in nature; you just see one form of energy changing into another form of energy, in nature time is cyclical. And somehow I think there's consolation for ageing poets to spend more time observing the minutest details out there."

In *Textures* we are witness to an ageing poet in fine form, but the energies of a younger sensibility are equally engrossing. Carefully structured and obviously well-researched, Muzanenhamo's poems in this collection are notably global in their reach. He stands out for his ability to transcend geographical and temporal boundaries and does so with apparent effortless dexterity: here the poems are set in the USA, UK, Norway, France, Peru, Mozambique, Somalia and Zimbabwe. "It fascinates me how similar people are," the poet explained, "You can go to any country and find we all possess the same emotions; perhaps we speak different languages, and there's a different landscape, but the baseline to all humanity strums at the same rhythm."

Muzanenhamo's focus is on what interests him, whether on his doorstep in Mashonaland or in Scandinavia, and whether it happened in the distant past or just recently. Despite such versatility, however, there is nevertheless a unifying style and a reassuring earthiness. His recent collection *Gumiguru* in fact shows remarkable skill in dealing more specifically with local Zimbabwean realities. Wherever the setting, a rural sensibility is never far; and we can imagine this tallies with Muzanenhamo's own life as a writer living on a farm.

Though the poems are primarily lyrical, they also tell stories, often about neglected persons or forgotten events. The 'Bluegrass Country' sequence, concerning the American jockey Isaac Murphy, arose from reading a book on art and racing. "He's one of the greatest jockeys of all time within America," said Muzanenhamo, "but very few people have heard of him. There's very little that's been said about the African-Americans who were racing around the end of the nineteenth century."

Murphy was initially buried with his wife Lucy. In the 1960s, as a supposed honour, his body was removed from his wife's side and reinterred next to Man o' War, one of the greatest thoroughbred racehorses. But it didn't end there; his body was moved twice thereafter. His grave can now be seen in the Kentucky Horse Park, outside of Lexington, but he's still separated from his wife. A contemplative speaker investigates this hidden history in a sequence uncovering irony and injustice.

Though Muzanenhamo is primarily an aural poet (most interested in musicality), his poems appeal also to visual stimuli in their various shapes. 'The Hamilton Piece', arranged on the page as it is, resembles an actual trophy, and we are also prompted to view the poet as an artist because there is a 'still-life' artistry to his work, an attempt to draw scenes, people and objects quietly and exactly – though through words that are used sparingly.

His speaker is also a 'fly on the wall', as in 'Gondershe', set amidst terrible conflict at the site of the ancient Somali coastal ruin, and introducing us to a boy, a would-be soldier, alone on a beach strewn with dead comrades, waiting for death himself. In its visual arrangement, the poem resembles the ebb and flow of waves crashing on a beach. The words, meanwhile, transport us directly to the scene: he "Wanted to scrawl his name in the sand./ Feel the tide tug at his nine year old heart./ And so he sat, quietly listening." Violence and killing are commonplace in several of the poems, yet the closeness to death allows Muzanenhamo to explore also what it means to be alive – what it has always meant, in any location or era.

In 'The Battle of Vågen', set in Norway in 1665, the theatre of war between Dutch and English fleets is observed in slow motion by a deserting young man who "abandoned pride and love and ran," leaving "a shy local girl" with whom he has already enjoyed life-affirming sex, to avoid pointless death and destruction. Such stories from across the globe, ancient and modern, uncover a human element in forgotten chapters of history.

I asked Muzanenhamo what gave rise to the 'Game of 12 Moons' sequence, which also traverses the globe and deals with the great themes of love, loss, war and death. "It was inspired by a recording by a classical composer, Luigi Nono," he explained, "I wrote the sequence quite quickly, over a period of a week. The piece that Nono had written [*No Hay Caminos, Hay Que Caminar*] was dedicated to the Russian director of *Solaris*, Andrei Tarkovsky. It's a powerful piece of music, with all these dark elements in it. That's what inspired 'Game of 12 Moons'." If the reader, without background knowledge, cannot at first access the meaning of these poems, it is nevertheless possible to appreciate their formal qualities, the moods they evoke, the assonance and alliteration, the profoundly affecting sounds.

I questioned the poets about their differences and Eppel said, "I think I'm a more subconscious poet. Togara uses a lot of his consciousness to craft his poems. I wake up, not with an idea, but an image or a rhythm, a structural rhythm, and then it grows into a poem. But 'Only Jacarandas', for example, just kind of came to me, as it was." While Eppel's work is frequently spontaneous, Muzanenhamo's is well researched and carefully planned (premeditated as it were). To this I would add what we have already established: the former is more focused on the local, while the latter is strikingly international in selecting subject matter. While Eppel still finds himself bound up in fraught yet apparently inescapable southern African identity politics (which inevitably shapes his poetry), this is not the case with Muzanenhamo who seems to embrace a more liberated attitude to poetic creativity, which is apparently now available to a younger, freer generation.

With their great attention to poetic craft, however, and their study of universal themes such as life and death, love and loss, the poets have many common concerns. Significantly, this collaboration challenges, in the words of Muponde and Primorac (2005: xviii), the "needless segregation of Zimbabwean literary traditions by 'race'"– which has been an unfortunate habit of the past. While there are interesting differences, all-in-all there is much to be gained from reading two of Zimbabwe's leading poets alongside one another.

References

Hughes, David McDermott. 2010. *Whiteness in Zimbabwe: Race, landscape and the problem of belonging*. New York: Palgrave

Merriam-Webster Dictionary. Definition of Poetry.
http://www.merriam-webster.com/dictionary/poetry

Muponde, Robert and Primorac, Ranka. 2005. 'Introduction', in Muponde and Primorac (eds.) *Versions of Zimbabwe: New Approaches to Literature and Culture*. Harare: Weaver Press

Wylie, Dan. 2012. 'Not Quite a Refutation: A Response to David McDermott Hughes's *Whiteness in Zimbabwe*', *Safundi: The Journal of South African and American Studies*, 13:1-2, 181-194, DOI: 10.1080/17533171.2011.644453

Note on the Book Cover

The connection between visual art and music is considered in the painting chosen for the book cover – Helen Lieros's *Homage to the Unknown* – which featured at the Gallery Delta's 'From Sound to Form' exhibition, and which depicts the third lament in Henryck Gorecki's Third Symphony. When the artist was studying music and her teacher asked, "What was that note?" she would respond with "blue" for F sharp and "red" for B Flat, having a sense that notes linked with colours; hence the resulting picture, apt also for an anthology of artistic and musical poetry.

Drew Shaw was born in Gweru in 1968, and studied in Canada, South Africa and the United Kingdom, obtaining his PhD in English from the University of London in 2004. He has long held an interest in Zimbabwean literature and wrote his PhD thesis on Dambudzo Marechera. Since then he has lectured at the School of Advanced Study at the University of London as well as Midlands State University and the National University of Science and Technology in Zimbabwe.

A Suburban Night in August

The distant all-night drum, a dripping tap,
a scops owl mimicking the creak of sap
rising. Dombeyas cream the bushy verge,
a tilted Southern Cross returns the surge
of hope in every second Hillside house.

The world is waiting, trembling like a mouse
as you, unconscious of the cricket's rasp,
in warm socks and striped pyjamas, unclasp
your hair, give it a tousle, set it free,
smiling at him the way you smiled at me.

Sonnet with a Limp

A million slaughtered doves fell from the sky,

soft-thudding, all around us – you

swaddled in Grandpa's shirt, stiffening, I

turning away from the thin blue

memory of your last reproachful look,

your death-nest of leaves like smashed beer

bottles, and the way the firmament shook

with plummeting birds. My hands smear

the distance so that my eyes can close in

on the hole you dug – harrying

things that scuttle – in anticipation

of this ashen day. Thus I sing

beloved pet, Louis, of doves falling,

grief, and disembodied voices calling.

Solvitur Ambulando*

I chose a night when the moon was high, chose
a time when bats from hell leathered the hairs
on the back of my neck, when guilty hose-
pipes coaxed honey from multi-petalled flairs;
a night for bawdy liars with scorched eyes
and only dark remembrances of suns
in the deepest of Bulawayo skies
where the Matseumhlope sewer runs;
I chose to solve it, not by talking
but by heeding the Saint, and walking,

walking. Moonlight changes shapes, so a cloud
of izintethe swarming the only
street light, is a shifting emerald shroud
of leaves; and a death-maiden, the lonely
spotted eagle owl blinking away tears,
blinking away recollections that, still,
like spitty bits, like words, like failed careers,
disturb me as I linger for the kill.
I'll choose to solve it not by talking
but by heeding the Saint, and walking,

walking. Changing shapes so that the shooting
star loses its trajectory, and falls
like Icarus, with helpless gums rooting

for his mother's tit. Rooftop caterwauls
muffle the dreadful splash of disregard.
C'est l'Ennui, the distracted poet cries,
grilled by beauty. The security guard
forgets to raise the alarm in surprise
at the sight of a white man walking,
who simply nods. He's done with talking.

* It is solved by walking (St Augustine)

Tortoise

You've been called a meat pie with a hard crust;
you learnt that life was not always unfair
when, against all odds, you vanquished the hare;
but you must endeavour to curb your lust.

Your shell's bestowed its name on feline dames;
your age, well that is anybody's guess:
much older than the pyramids but less
durable than plectrums, spectacle frames,

and old ladies' combs. An appetizer
for neo-colonialists, they plunge
you, live, into boiling water, expunge
your role as bearer of the earth, as the

symbol of involution, a return
to immateriality, music
of the spheres resonating, buzzing, click-
click clicking... not a word ... helped Kurma churn

the Sea of Milk, helped Kung Kung deposit
the celestial pillar, helped secure
the isles of the immortals, helped ensure,
'with odd old ends stol'n forth of holy writ',

That those who commemorate sight and sound–

poets, composers, and picture-makers–

will complete the work of undertakers,

and begin the work of he, 'who with his finger wrote on the ground'.

Only Jacarandas

Willows require still pools,
girls, silver-backed mirrors,
priests, the cross of Jesus.

Only jacarandas
can take their reflection
from the dull sky of tarmac.

The Hillside Dams in Bulawayo: A Sonnet Sequence

Aloes at Hillside Dams

There is something human about aloes.

They smell – and feel, if you probe the slimy

parts – like sex. They have cuticular roots

and they object to being planted in rows.

Their welcome is arm-like, sometimes grimy

with white scale, sometimes polished absolutes.

Their process of dying is shameless: top

down (or bottom up). In their multitudes

they elaborate these Dams, not, somehow,

as genus, or variety, or crop,

but as comrades, citizens, darlings, dudes.

Their spaced teeth are not vicious. Then and now,

past and present, something human. The name

invites a greeting… all winter… aflame.

Beauty is Truth, Truth Death

When I negotiate rocks that divide
and unite upper and lower dams, I
feel that I'm being taken for a ride
on some lopsided insect, a moth fly,
perhaps, or a dark, predaceous water
beetle, tilted, not by geology
but by wind, a regular ripsnorter
at this time of seasonal change; a free-
for-all, between your legs, between liquid
upper and solidifying lower;
earth and sea; there on the threshold, a bid
not to prayer but to pleasure; a knower
finally, of the truth: beauty is death.
So. Put down your pen and take a deep breath.

Giving up on the Rains in Curious Rhyme

When leaves, skittering across tarmac, sound

like empty cans strung behind a wedding

car; when the day feels papery enough

to go up in flames; when the devil thorn,

harder and sharper than a girl's tight lip,

not only punctures my bicycle tyre

but engraves lonely hearts on window panes;

when king crickets evacuate the ground

because grass has forgotten how to sing,

how to accommodate billy goat gruff,

his nanny, kids born and yet to be born;

when the knot of longing's too tight to slip

under stones that crackle like fat on fire,

I put down my pen, give up on the rains.

Looking for You

I walk the pet we shared. We look for you

under the giant monkey thorn that fell,

taking half a kopje with it; pursue

squirrels that might or might not expel

the longing, canine and human. We climb

above the stink of dirty socks, the fret

of humus, to a granite view sublime

(in the old sense). I must will to forget,

if forgetting can be willed. She nuzzles

me, eager to resume our hopeless quest,

past that orange bench where the num-num spills

its blossom. At the Upper Dam we'll rest

where the dead bodies of platanna bloat,

and two discarded beer bottles float.

Not For Laura*

The lower dam thickens like simmering

soup as the season for showers recedes

into the blue. The emerging sun bleeds

like a bushfire, red alert, shimmering

on the nutrient slime. Hopeful frogs sing

of spawning times to come. Coral tree seeds

may germinate into bracelets of beads.

Updraughts unsettle a dragon fly's wing.

Last night I heard a border collie howl,

a sparrow-weaver muttered in its nest;

last night the blue moon brought you back to me,

your smile at first, receding to a scowl.

I'm not progressive, I have failed the test:

bin kein bonobo, *bin echt* chimpanzee.

*Petrarch's muse

Gondershe

Having never fired a gun before, he held the rifle
as though the weapon were a dying child about to say something
only they could share,
the sea quietly unfurling surf and salt into a prayer
he had once heard his mother's voice sink into.
The ruin behind him echoed with moonlight, the moon
falling back over his shoulder, silver and heavy like a slow missile.
They were all dead – the men of the sand,
the men who knew the make of helicopters by the cut of the blades.
He'd been told of the sea by them and wanted to hear its cool salt whispers.
Wanted to scrawl his name on the shore.
Feel the tide tug at his twelve-year-old heart.
And so he sat, alone, quietly listening,
cradling the rifle in his arms, a faint line beginning to part sky from sea.
The smell of burning diesel growing strong.
Come the dawn there would be no escape.
He would die. Even the sea would burn.

Peruvian Sunsets

"I felt disturbed, my nerves on edge; it seemed as though someone was emptying a box of pins into my brain..."

Clemente Palma

Xalvadora stumbled back after Alvaro removed his boots. It wasn't that Alvaro's foot was metallic, nor was it the foot's cold mercurial glow that caused her to panic and suddenly retreat with fear; no – it wasn't that at all. When Xalvadora looked down again at Alvaro's bloodless ankle, she saw her own face staring back: her dark eyes, wasted and hollow. She turned away. Alvaro's warm, soft fingers fell gently on her bare shoulders, his palms hot on her skin. Her breath fell back. She stared over the park where the setting sun cooled like doused bronze. The modern world was quietly turning dark. She could smell cigar smoke on his breath. Her knees dipped as she thought of the warmth of his tongue.

They stood still for a while. Her eyes searching the view. Rows of twisted olive trees faded black into the evening. *Why him?* she thought – his sullen cheeks sucking into his jaws, his dark earthy beard collapsing like a shallow grave. He locked his fingers over her belly, the rough skin of his hairy arms all freckled and brown like dirty tallow. She looked down at the park. People still sat on benches. Neon lights began to flitter and spit over tall iron fences, the retiring commerce sweet with the flow of electric light, the city's heavy salt air thinning with a chill. *But where had all the doves gone?* Without absolute resignation of light, she couldn't tell time from the date, she felt... *everywhere at once in one constant place.* Terrible thoughts hung on memories of the sea where breakers rose to be flung

back off rock like prayer. Could Alvaro have known how the old city's naked walls had haunted her all her life, how every star splintered violently in her dreams? The olive trees came to life again with the soft lighting in the park. Wine glasses on the windowsill cradled a universe of stars, the cold colloquial wind swirling with the sound of traffic. She could feel his penis throbbing hot and hard, a tight angry knot weeping into the small of her back. He pressed his weight harder against her skin. His sweet, smoky breath boiling deep in the atoll of her collarbone. As streetlights withdrew the burden of time, she casually turned. Kissed him. Lips, hard against his. Mouth, flat against his mouth.

The Texan

"James A. Mattern, noted flier, was granted permission by the Commerce Department today to make an aerial search for the Russian aviators believed lost in the Arctic wilderness.

In making the search, Mr. Mattern will be returning a favor from Sigismund Levanevsky, leader of the Russian flight.

The Russian went to Mr. Mattern's rescue a few years ago when the American aviator was marooned in Northern Siberia."

Pittsburg Post-Gazette, **August 15, 1937**

From Weeks Field the sun hangs uncertain,

the air sharpened by the curse of razored winds –

sheets of sky and sea layered silver with ice.

Each hour vanishes into broken distances,

the shape of the world formed on each breath, oiled drops

shivering wet off rivets – the engine

moaning dark at the wrists.

Evening swivels west as the Texan turns,

her wings banked shallow above the ocean's crust –

pedals and levers at their place for altitude.

Through angled glass, the quiet world of a frozen

solitude, a vast naked bridge of bruised light bridging continents,

white skirts of blind speed beaming

over lengths of desolate prose.

The radio crackles white with endless noise,

        the ceiling of the world dry with fate.

And banking into the failing light, he remembers the furled

        wisps sparked by whips of air turning up as the Russian landed –

then, the rattled chop of blades as the plane left for Nome,

        the compass marked for home and all

        the vaporous qualities of life.

Time sinks fast, darkening with ancient layers

        creaking below, unsaid prayers the dead

have set to verse. A grey breath of air slips heavily

        off each wing, the flat drone of the engine working

the mind to paint the final flight with a grieved art – the soul's white feathers

        burning bright as the prototype rolled and crashed

        deep into the heart of the unknown.

The Art of Man

"Even if the word genius was used as sparingly as it should be, the late nineteenth and early twentieth century jeweler René Lalique would always be so described. Rather than a craftsman with a leaning toward the artistic, he was an accomplished artist who chose to express himself primarily in jewelry."

Geoffrey Munn, *The Magazine ANTIQUES*

"A flighted full toss on leg stump by a spinner. Any other will play this shot on leg side by pull shot or glance or flick. But Sachin made a space and played a perfect cover drive for four."
Martin Crowe, cricketer

The signature phrase: the trumpet's brass crescendo
rises bright over chirping clarinets. Michael Aspel,
BBC professional, stands in front of a castle in Wales.
A brief introduction displays the grandeur of Powys.
How do they keep the grass so fuckin' green! The ball
turning slowly through the screen, over intact bales –

back to the keeper squatting on his heels. Jackman
comments on the seam after a wry remark by Shastri.
*He began his glassmaking career making perfume
bottles for the Corsican perfumer Coty, I assume
around about… 1910, but this is earlier. The artistry
is truly breathtaking. How did such a piece come*

into your possession? A fingernail gently nudges
a brooch. A woman, battling out of the 20th century
takes her time with words. *You fuckin' god Tendulkar!*
A single run off the second ball of the fiftieth over,

history, a double ton! *And that's real gold? Really?*
Yes. The insect's body is formed from pâte de verre,

the wings from plique-à-jour enamel. The innings
done. *They can't expect to chase this down.* The art,
the clean, learned finish – 25 fours, 3 sixes, *faster*
than any man! The absolute quality of a true master
at work. In the background some intellectual fart
in a purple knitted cardigan nods sternly, laughter

emanates somewhere far off in the hall. Everyone
knows the outcome; the local crowd sensing victory;
the glass cicada's polished fire flying over the deck
at Gwalior. *If this went up for auction – this Lalique…*
No, she stops him. Something about family history
falls flash-lit with ticker tape over a cardboard cheque.

♥

Uzziah Chikambi woke, put on his jeans then got the shotgun. *Mogo doesn't bark for nothing,* was the first thought to enter his mind. Uzziah crouched at the door, and as he listened, a strange feeling ran through him, an emotion he had not felt before. *Best stay in,* he thought, but something urged him to go out there. So when he stepped out into the night and saw the strange light

shivering in his field, he knew something was wrong. The light sat pale and wounded. Uzziah chambered a shell. The shotgun cool and heavy in his arms. And for a while, he simply stood there. Without warning, the pale light shot up silently, high above his head, hung, shifted, then crashed in a neighbouring field on Beste Farm, where it rested, weak. Now Uzziah did something strange –

he began to walk to the light, the crisp air wired with a strange metallic charge. He felt nervous, but the closer he got to the light the calmer he became. Mogo, light-footed with ease, did her best to keep up with Uzziah, who now swaggered with the shotgun casually balanced on the brace of his arm. And as he walked, his heels rolled nakedly into a dark illustrated echo where there

could be nothing else but shadows living in the music of their own fear. He now found himself on a street, above him – a strange visceral mass hung like a womb. From the thick-muscled sack, his father emerged – naked, eyes burning in the cold sunlight, *'DO U ♥ NY?'* a slow towering voice asked. The policeman's gun made him nervous, so he knew to hold his tongue. At the best of times he was not good with words, and this was not the best of times. He looked up at the man mounted on the horse, their eyes met, shivering back and forth. Uzziah then felt the shotgun slip back into his grip – its black weight locked with a strange intensity, dark like reversed fire. From above, a volt of hot light broke over the city's concrete grid, a blaze of heat bathed his

face in white electrified ash. An aching knot blossomed in his heart. Every triumph flowered wild with every regret, the best and worst of his life. The mounted officer pointed to a light blue Delphos gown draped over an old municipal bench, their two year-old son stiff in the cradled shade. This cruel, strange apparition forced a trail of tears down his face... The shotgun

coughed twice!! The aftertaste of the sun warm on his lips. There were bestial screams everywhere, sirens rose before a strange light gave way to everything but the blunt sound of another gun.

Desire

"There is something where things have to have a certain consistency, but don't ask
me what this consistency is." György Ligeti

1964, off Lourenço Marques

It felt good being back on the water,
    the reflection of the midmorning sun twisting off his face.
He sat at the helm and stared ahead –
the pulpit's railings burning bright above the prow,
the yacht ploughing its slow liquid song through the channel.
For twelve long years he'd longed to view the world as it was now –
a warm expanse of freedom,
            a vast canvas of blues loosely folding over pallid greens.
He closed his eyes, purged his mind of any thought of land.
    And prayed.

        *

When he opened his eyes, he saw Noémia standing in the pulpit
wearing his dress shirt – the large white sleeves rolled up to her elbows,
    the hem fluttering over her dark naked thighs.
Her hair, thick and sun bleached, cast a mopped shadow over her brow.
Noémia cradled a coffee mug in her hands and stared off into the distance
where the sky merged with the sea, where distance and air unified colour.
    The heat began to settle and sit heavy on the water.
    He tied off the tiller, everything slowing down as the air thickened.
As he looked at Noémia, a fleeting fragment of music entered his mind –
    oboe and cello, the notes drawn rich and deep.

22

He closed his eyes,

working and reworking the phrase, varying the oboe around the cello,

the arrangement becoming clearer and clearer –

the music flowing with the gentle lull of waves washing off the prow.

And as he drew deeper

within himself, each note became darker, heavier. Beautiful.

He clicked his fingers and looked up, but Noémia was gone.

Something swirled deep within him. His chest tightened. His breath thinned –

drawing his body into a vortex

that spun into a tail of silence.

When he came to, he lay on his back, his face to the sky.

The tiller creaking between the ropes.

He could taste blood in his mouth as he lifted himself to his feet.

He stood there for a while, recovering, thinking of nothing –

the arcane sky mirroring the sea's marbled greens.

He stood, staring over the vast expanse of water where a shape began to grow.

A distant ship.

Or a huge black bird.

*

The yacht's stem cut through the ocean with its ancient music.

The sun ate his skin as he lowered himself from the bowsprit.

With one foot lashed to the short projection,

he ran his hand through the bow wave,

saltwater clean off his wrist – the air, a warm whisper.

In the emerald depths, shadows appeared and vanished without warning –
great flat shapes like immersed continents travelling at speed.
As he hung there, watching the flat liquid shadows,
      he hoped Noémia would find him staring into the depths –
            a crazed visionary speaking to the sea.
But as he thought of her coming up on deck
      to find him with his foot lashed to the bowsprit,
            chest pressed flat to the prow,
he also thought of how her face would melt at the sight of him
shouting into the water – so he pulled himself up,
            back onto the deck where he sat motionless in the sun.
            And wept.

*

When he entered the forepeak,
      he found Noémia asleep.
A warm breeze slithered sluggishly through the berth.
      She lay naked in the heat,
half on her stomach, half on her flank –
her black buttocks glistening like crude oil.
      He stood still and watched her,
his round silhouette filling the entrance to the berth –
the slow mantra of creaking wood
      rolling, creaking, rolling.
      His breaths deepening.
His need to descend on her
      spiralling out of control.

Cape Turtle Dove

for Brenda Page

I've seen you do it on the road,
I've smelt you turning on a spit;
I understand the twitcher's code...
but that's not it.

I touched you once, your bobbing head,
observed you sorting seeds and grit,
noticed that your eyes aren't red...
but that's not it.

An open woodland takes your shape,
near water, where you love to sit,
shades of lavender on your nape...
but that's not it.

Your noisy flap, your half-ringed neck,
your gentle manner – not a bit –
your warning rasp, your vicious peck...
but that's not it.

Your song. Your distant, haunting call,
like well-loved landscapes lately lit;
three syllables that rise and fall...
and that's it.

Grey Heron

He sports a neatly tailored coat of mouse
pelts, his legs are fragile, like a feather-
weight's in the ringside glare, or the windscreen
wipers of an omnibus in the dry
season. He keeps to himself like some poets
and, like some poets, he refuses to wear
a tie, though he will sometimes fold his neck
as neatly as any odd stocking. He
surprised me today, as motionless as
a guerrilla in an ambush, bill poised
for the kill. On one leg he conjures up
a notion of contemplation. He roosts
at Borrow Street baths on the very edge
of the colony. Phoenix bird, don't perch
on my house before I've had it re-wired.

Hornbills in My Garden

Reborn I am among the hungry ghosts;
again I hear the hornbill's plaintive cry;
attended to once more by all the hosts
of heaven and of hell. 'Cast a cold eye'
says the poet, but I am too attached.
Hornbills by the number have come crying
into town; yellow-grey and dusty, hatched
in coffins of mopane wood, flying
high then dipping like soup ladles; crashing
bashing in the branches tall, calling... call
me to the table, serve me, kiss me, sing
to me. God have mercy on me, and all
he has to disobedience consigned,
and don't forget to kill me once I've dined.

Bronze Mannikins

I feel my atoms expanding,
not like bubble wrap
or dumplings
or inner tubes,
but like tiny birds,
tiny twittering birds
with purplish heads,
iridescent green
shoulder patches,
and long black tails.
There's a fluttering in my heart.

I feel my atoms contracting,
not like wet shirt sleeves
or English sausages
or popped balloons,
but like tiny birds,
tiny twittering birds
dropping like leaves,
cuddling up close,
squeezing into communal nests,
smothering the bird table.
There's a quivering in my heart.

Brown-Hooded Kingfisher

Your hyperbolic beak has mesmerised
you – you glaze past poems, past the abyss
of waters. You have been immobilized
by instinct, by a chronic state of bliss.

You once fished in waters above the sky,
in the firmament of death and desire.
There is a witness, who can testify,
a priest; he observed you catching fire

like a church window at sunrise – Della
Robbia blue; Blessed Virgin Mary,
Mother of God, of the Word, of Stella
and her baby boy – *right now, unwary*

of my savage cat. Impossible beak,
orange legs, reddish feet glued to a tree;
Dickensian eyebrows, unnerving shriek
shadowed by a gentling, 'pity for me'.

Scrub Robin

1

I'm not reclining beneath a plum tree
on Hampstead Heath; I'm not about to fade
into oblivion. True, I can't see
what's going on about my feet displayed
in the season's first mud. They say the act
of observation changes whatever
is observed. Does that apply to birdsong?
Can sound be seen? Cool seepage soothes my cracked
heels as I, a Friday's child, endeavour
to locate it bob, bob, bobbin' along.

2

Then, it was Mopani scrub, that odour
of turpentine; the obliterating
chorus of cicadas; and always her
smoke-filled hours… lipstick, powdered cheeks… waiting
for the man with gorilla arms, and eyes
like cornflowers. Or singeing the firm-set
small feathers of a plump hen with the flames
from a twisted newspaper. Lullabies
to shoot the moon, to learn the alphabet;
counting – 1,2,3,4,5 – counting games.

3

In the morning, in the evening, rockin'
robin. Wrapping his flask of sweet, milky
tea with my Ouma's old Lisle stocking,
or part of the same newspaper, which she
used to singe the chicken, and which he reads
after work, on the stoep, from the back page
to the news, glass of Mainstay in his fist.
Ouma, vamping ain't we got fun, feeds
the cat on cream crackers, recalls her stage
debut in the roaring twenties, much missed.

4

Unlike the scrub robin that tweets the sun
when it rises and when it sets, she trips
to moonlit memories (one, two, three) of fun-
filled years after Delville Wood, while Mom strips
bed linen, and Dad files his fingernails,
and I, red mud squelching between my toes,
examine sickle bush thickets for eggs,
transforming whatever I observe: dales
into dongas, leas into bushveld, prose
into uncertain rhymes, lees into dregs.

5

Counting syllables while Dad remembers
Tobruk... rockin' robin... El Alamein...
white dust on his boots, hot desert embers
still glowing. Mom, tightly folding the pain
with her arms. Where will the cigarette ash
fall? Where will I find an untidy cup
of grass with protruding stems, neat lining,
and two freckled eggs? Suddenly a flash,
low-flying, skulking, you could say. Look up,
look down – gone. But listen to it pouring

6

forth its soul like moonlight when a fleeting
girl, colleen, lovely woman, took my hand
and placed it on a heart that stopped beating
for me when it stopped for her. Understand
that the act of observation alters
whatever is observed. I thought I saw
its tail, briefly, fanned, but it could have been
the detached wing of a moth, or the burrs
on a bush baby's rump, or a shrew's claw,
slightly curved, almost too small to be seen.

7

The mud has dried in scabs upon my feet;
I count the days, I count the minutes too;
I like to fantasize, to guess each sweet,
to wonder how I lost a girl like you;
but where's the use, this light-forsaken day,
of moaning like the wind that comes between
the song of dawn, the song of dusk... trilling
robin... of saying I loved you? Away!
Don't go! Away! I can't know what you mean:
observing eyes above cracked cheeks, spilling;

8

eyes seeping tears for what? For midnight?
I wonder if Ruth heard you in that field,
if she ever discerned the stripes, the white
tips, the rufous rump; and awake, I yield,
asleep, I yield, to whatever avails:
what I hear, what I see, and what I think
I know, is that the song of dusk, and dawn,
in this brown land is not the nightingale's
but the scrub robin's, and there is a link
holding what is cheerful and what forlorn.

Saboteurs

"I'll win the Tour de France provided I'm not murdered before we get to Paris."
Maurice Garin, 1904

«*Nous fussions morts pour Dreyfus. Dreyfus n'est point mort pour Dreyfus.*»
Charles Péguy, *Notre Jeunesse*

This is their country,
Saint-Étienne, Annonay, Lyon,
    their mountain pass –
Col de La République now waging war on us –
their folk hard on the road
pumping fists, baying for blood –
    our bodies wrenched tight to our machines,
gear and chain turning heavy with time.
To love their own is for the sake of death,
    and strangers will drive the civic wheel
to that cause, a fevered heat
    wet with fervour.
Lyon had seen us in to club-wielding hoodlums,
        brass knuckles polished with spit.
When morning came to the fore
    with ceremony and flags –
        beer and wine flowed
to get us over the pass, through the mobs,
over iron tacks and broken glass –
elbows tucked back defending our ribs.

Through the black violent tunnel,
the call of names fired wild with betrayal –
            words ripe with rage,
      till shots sounded.
            The mob cleared and fled –
leaving their man to vanish up the road,
      disappearing over the col
fuelled by the blood of his city, his heart surging
for all its worth, breath owed to the land's history –
            just as those who forged the heavy
      templates to set the aged press
                  and print the dark pages
            to scourge another race.

The Battle of Vågen

Bergen, Norway – August 3, 1665

After the church bells

    echoed in Bergen Bay, Gerritsz stole off

the cargo fluyt and made for the city's temporal walls,

Biggita's door bolted back, not in denial

but fear. For days they'd watched the ships come in,

        cordon the neutral bay,

            seamen loud on the streets,

liquored up and lusty.

    When the bells rang, and drums rolled

and heads bowed for what would come, Gerritsz

abandoned love and pride and ran. Thorn

    and stone bloodied his gentle hands,

        weeding his path up

            the scrubland of Fløyen.

From the mountain top

    he saw the merchant ships pinned back,

the leeward gunners lined beside the Bergenhus,

the Dutch positioned, giving their broadsides.

        He had never seen real war,

      and had no will to die; only

            two weeks before

he'd found himself fucking
    a shy local girl – smuggling pouches
of nutmeg and mace to each of their trysts.
He felt alive. His mind stained with her naked
    image, he was lost in the sweetness
of her lips and wished never to return
        to the dull life of Dordrecht.

In the bay below he watched
the theatre of war begin like a board game,
    his heart surged to keep pace with his pulse.
Cannon fire thundered with the heavy vibrato of war.
    From his vantage point he could see the crafts
shivering after bouts of light hung
        long then rang with distant noise.

In his mind, the thought
    of men dying could not be reconciled
with what he viewed. Rain coursed down his face
salted with tears he could not hold back,
    the shame of running, the fear
of loving. And now that he had found love –
    the fear of wanting love.

He watched the ships.
    The dirty flames. The harbour turning black.
Falling to his knees amid weak ferns, he swore
he would not return to Dordrecht. So he rose,
    turned from the view
        and walked north
        into the southern rain.

Religion

Where dolphins congregate,

darkness journeys in the wake of folktales –

we were making history

deep within each breath,

our names losing light,

the rocks almost forgotten.

Bluegrass Country

for E.W-A

"In about 70 years, you can place my body here"
Eddie Arcaro, the reinterment of Isaac Murphy, Faraway Farm, Lexington, 1967

"One more mighty plunge, and with knee, limb and hand,
I lift my horse first by a nose past the stand.
We are under the string now – the great race is done
And Salvator, Salvator, Salvator won!"
Ella Wheeler Wilcox, 'How Salvator Won'

Isaac Murphy: *1861 – 1896*

I.   Churchill Downs
              1891

Furlongs of sky curve fast over burning rails –

dirt thundering and flicking up beneath the polished clap of sweat.

At the reins, each breath draws bluntly from the sternum.

Knees in. The sun ringing loud. Pumped fists and hats tipped to wave wild

from the grandstand – a roaring applause

composed of timeless stuff: men bowed hard, given to the mane,

the short whistled catch of leather on sculpted folds of flesh.

As the sky bends out straight,

speed is held –

man and horse flat out,

the weight of flames shivering in the eyes

of rider and beast,

breaths of fire

spilling wet

off lips of the fevered crowd.

Togara Muzanenhamo

II.   Cemetery of the Union Benevolent Society
             1955

Tangled vines breathe over cooling backs of stone,
sun-veined nut sedge bound tight over dates eroded by time.
   The earth rests wired and neglected. Another summer comes to pass.
The dead lie without names here, the link of age rusted with ankle chains
                    running quiet into a fog of clouded musket fire.
     The railroad sings loud over junkyard metal twisted by sunlight.
Beyond a trodden fence, Lexington sits forged by southern prayer –
         Baptist words rising from the heart,
                 burdened songs sung
          for the leaden-paced march into each quick-silvered twilight
             reined by the whip's black hymn,
               songs sung by those
                   who'd walked the dark
             roads only to learn
               to run, then ride alone.

III.   The Hamilton Piece
           1980

From

Jordan's Row

this slow silver light

stands solid in its place,

a laboured

gleam

sloping off narrow shoulders

with an unassumed grace;

rider

standing sure

and strong,

jacket and

crop

in hand,

knee-high

boots,

long

legs

plant-

ing

a

silver

stride

set firm

on the base of the American equine turf.

IV.   Charging Shadow
          Circa 1964

Always this dream, the
immortal flick of wind,
the dark sediment caking
our mouths. Always this
feeling of time sitting flat
like crust turning soft in
our brains – the earth
wet with a dour embrace.
Wandering footfall tears
through the union of fo-
liage and sun, a breath of
earth and stone thicken-
ing with an inquisitive
charge. How do the dead
defend themselves, cross-
armed, hollow-breasted,
muscle undone by the
wet-rotting song of time.
For years we lay lost,
hugged tight by mounds
of ungoverned earth,
squat nameless blocks
knotted above our heads
till the shovel's eye sunk
its blade and tipped and
rose with pure betrayal.

V.   The Ungiving

And for a while, the darkness is new again,
      the earth heavy with the ungiving spring.
      Who will hear the gentle spats of rain
spit on earth and turn songs we'd forgotten to singing
            hymns rooted to trees sweet
            with the blood of pinioned fruit,
            fruit hung from boughs, swinging
      swollen and ripe, casually falling
                  beyond the view of this plain.

VI.   Faraway Farm, Lexington
            1967

Lucy Murphy: 1868 – 1910

The mineral sound of bone rings heavy
with each natural layer of calcium, the wind
sweeping low with Kentucky's prayers.
Paddocks and fields roll out to naked views
where troubled mares slip off to foal
the sun over fresh snow, the moon setting

            again, drawing me to think of you.

                In simple terms, light is inverted,
                the air folded to compact earth –
                the world another place, another life
                where veined roots are cut blind –
                the white thread of matrimonial love
                severed from the jasmine bone.

And so the seat is rich, yet the throne
                quiet on the template of legendary
worth, a wealth of praise bowing with
                the humility of stone. And where
time sits is far divorced from the heart,
                the air damp with bone set beneath
dust and snow; the matter of flesh

resolved by the earth, the matter of us
     turned again, incomplete by the vogue
        of time, my head in your arms forgotten,
the chalkstone dirt stretch heavy with calcium,
        the track drumming hard with hoof and applause,
the grief of Kentucky's prayers, the black-foaled
        stars giddy where our hearts lay
      quiet in the brier-tangled shadows,
the music of unwanted distance grating loud
      with what can only be
        the memory of an intimate age.

VII.   Call to the Post
         2011
                              Kentucky Horse Park

The memorial stands to crown Man o' War,
        Secretariat sired by distant blood,
                royal stakes and garlands
                trickling dew to gather
        where each chestnut colt stands
proud, dawn folding back its copper hood.

The light is simple. Each quiet, warm stable
        heavy with the tang of manure,
                blue starlings whistling,
                the air fresh with subtle
        notes, perfumes and light falling
heavier and heavier on this portrait of nature

carved into art with patient hands of a dream,
        a dream tended with a gardener's
                care. Red iron seals the kiss
                of fire rising with steam,
        the farrier's wrist turning after a hiss
of heat, memories forged from water: winners

wreathed heavy with roses – each fired petal
        bright as the sun. But all that's gone,
                and all that's left is the fresh
                perfume, the subtle
        notes of brass songs over retired flesh,
the angled sun on a name etched deep in stone.

Dorothy Recollects

[a pastiche]

Lingering with Coleridge in the garden; pulled a basket of peas,
and broiled Coleridge a mutton chop. The beauty of the moon
was startling as it rose to us. Bowels bad.

A thorough wet day. Baking and starching. Coleridge ate nothing
to cure his boils. Copied poems for the LB. William
out of spirits. I read German till late.

The moonshine like herrings in the water. Coleridge had a sweet day
for his ride... dear dear fellow. At last I eased my heart by
weeping. Nervous blubbering, William says.

I stayed at home and clapped the small linen. Mended William's stockings
while he worked at The Ruined Cottage and made himself ill.
I went to the other bed with tooth-ache.

A heart-rending letter from Coleridge. Mary and William walked
to the Boat House at Rydal. Every horned cow
puts me in terror. Took laudanum.

An unusual softness in the prospect – a rich yellow
upon the fields, a soft grey purple on the waters. The clouds
were moveless. Made me more than half a poet.

John Eppel

William worked at the cuckow poem. I sewed beside him.
The fire flutters, the watch ticks. I hear nothing else save
 the breathing of my beloved. A blessed hour.

I must wash myself then off. No letters! I expected one
fully from Coleridge. But as I climbed the Moss, the moon came out.
O the unutterable darkness

of the sky and the earth below the moon. It gave me exquisite
feelings. I got tea when I reached home. Read Spenser
while he made a pillow of my shoulder.

A cropped ash with upright forked branches like the Devil's horns
frightening a guilty conscience. William observed that the full moon
above a dark fir grove's a fine image

of the descent of a superior being. On Monday
my brother William was married to Mary Hutchinson.
William had parted from me upstairs.

I gave him the wedding ring – with how deep a blessing. He took it
from my forefinger where I had worn it the whole of the night before.
He slipped it again onto my finger

and blessed me fervently. I kept myself as quiet as I could,
but when it was over I could stand it no longer and threw
myself on the bed where I lay in stillness.

I prevailed upon William to go up with me to the ruins.
We left Mary sitting by the kitchen fire. Poor Mary!
William fell asleep lying upon my breast.

Near fainting and very bad in my bowels. Put books in order,
put aside dear C's letters. I walked out, my head aching.
The moon hung like a gold ring snapped in two.

I have been beside him ever since tea, repeating some of his
sonnets, listening to his own repeating, reading Milton's.
Mary is in the parlour, baking cakes.

Golden Orb Spider

Can't get that dangling girl out of my mind,
nor the jealousy that provoked it. Why
are pampered Olympians so unkind
to mortals who challenge them, vivify
them in the first place? Athene, mistress
of weaving, versus the Lydian wench,
Arachne, who dares to make Olympus
say yes to human pain. How do the French
put it: *la Terre détruit le Ciel?**
It's a story Sartre might want to tell.

Yes, 'might want to'. In the orb spider's web
Mozart is still composing. The golden
yellow staves of silken moonlight flow, ebb,
ebb, flow… spiralling… while, not beholden
to anyone, Dambudzo's zigzag script
shocks and enthrals, half pretending to be
a/part; and sun-drunk Vincent, one ear ript
like Hardy's rotten rose, striving to free
pigment from shapes, paints numerous haystacks,
gets hold of someone's revolver, and cracks.

Yes, the sadness will last forever; so
will the joy; especially when an early
morning dew transforms the fine meshed halo,
transforms the urgent desire to *be*
into silvery threads among the gold:
sticky memory and dry forgetting;
indeed, my children, I am growing old,
confused. Thanks, Mrs Spider, for letting…
…Nephila, with your inward pointing tips,
weave me the dear red curve of her lips;

weave me the aquamarine of her eyes;
weave me the gift of a shawl for her head;
weave me her honey-pale look of surprise
when she learns that the dead bury the dead.
Can't get it out of my mind, the tangling
word, nor the image of the snake you trapped,
nor the seed-eating bird you've been mangling,
and all the lesser creatures you have sapped.
Thank you for letting me experience
what I don't understand but what I sense.

*the Earth destroys the Heavens

Compass

The scene is set, the girl is wet,
a strand of hair across her mouth;
the dripping eaves, the soggy leaves –
a boy approaching from the south.

Her eyes are grey, her ears are fey,
with rocking hips she bodies forth;
her navel smells of silent bells –
a boy approaching from the north.

Her breasts are curved, her nipples nerved,
her sex a sulky palimpsest;
her blighted toes in occult rows –
a boy approaching from the west.

The scene is set, the girl is wet,
she signals to suspend the feast;
the soggy leaves, the dripping eaves –
a boy approaching from the east.

Four Villanelles

1

Davids are Goliaths in waiting –
the corrupting effect of power
it's a maxim worth re-stating

re-considering re-contemplating
they kidnap then they deflower
Davids are Goliaths in waiting

listen to their molars grating
as they disembowel devour
it's a maxim worth re-stating

forced fellating forced mating
let the bitches cower
Davids are Goliaths in waiting

make them ululate make them sing
make their sweetness sicken to sour
it's a maxim worth re-stating

bring back our girls bring them back bring
break the steeple the rod the tower
Davids are Goliaths in waiting
it's a maxim worth re-stating

2

absinthe makes the heart grow fonder
tulips brushing against his thighs
many times dead La Gioconda

many times dead the greening yonder
wormwood wormwood the actor sighs
absinthe makes the heart grow fonder

the first glass is a glass of wonder
the second glass is a glass of lies
many times dead La Gioconda

not the last soft giant to squander
genius on go-lightly guys
absinthe makes the heart grow fonder

afternoon's a time to ponder
bilious dames and emerald skies
many times dead La Gioconda

write no libel speak no slander
spare him from the worldly-wise
absinthe makes the heart grow fonder
many times dead La Gioconda

3

blood is stickier than water
red of the evening black of the night
my son my son my daughter

mingling after the slaughter
emptying the holy grail of light
blood is stickier than water

forfeits of gold frankincense and myrrh
a pitying and a pitiful sight
my son my son my daughter

seeping through rubble of bricks and mortar
putting his renegades to flight
blood is stickier than water

in a vespertine glow I sought her
but she had gone with her questing knight
my son my son my daughter

the day he appeared to court her
she became his acolyte
blood is stickier than water
my son my son my daughter

4

you need light to cast a shadow
slavery gave birth to the blues
you need things dead to make things grow

a dashed ember's darkening glow
persecution availed the Jews
you need light to cast a shadow

roses pruned make the sweetest show
why do others' mishaps amuse
you need things dead to make things grow

ashes flicker when breezes blow
the losers win the winners lose
you need light to cast a shadow

swing high my darling child swing low
 put on your hat kick off your shoes
you need things dead to make things grow

the seasons come the seasons go
this old man is paying his dues
you need light to cast a shadow
you need things dead to make things grow

Engine Philosophers

The smell of steel and oil is the incense of our labour.

    In fields shot green with growth, brittle with grain,

or bare as anvils – we extend our hands over the iron altar.

Sometimes visions are lost through the slip of a spanner,

    a misplaced nut collapses a thought like a faulty jack.

But no real workman worth his salt jumps in straight off the bat

to rotate a shaft or turn a bolt. Down to changing a wheel,

a moment's silence honours an established principle.

Tractors, trailers, bowsers and sumps, planters, gauges,

    hydraulic pumps worked by drivers of different ages,

from different owners of different sexes, all contribute in sync

to at least three Arcadian laws governing modern mechanics.

    Sweet milky tea does the rounds. Discourse begins.

Here is where the poses of hands-in-pockets and fists-on-chins

perfected the way a solemn frown holds a solemn thought.

Here real thinkers never smear oil, from worked engines,

between thumb and forefinger; that's just not done

    beneath galvanised roofs of workshops or the bare

punishing slap of the sun. Not real thinkers! Something European

makes us want to speak German. And through the common

    phrase about all knowledge being interpretation –

cogwheels and chains turn in our heads. Consideration

changes down to movement. Old tools of knowledge, worked

and scarred, gleam flatly with the nature of honest work.

All the Good Help

He will not understand her fascination
with rain, these summer months of water
that somehow keep the money coming in,
paying for the nurses his granddaughter

has slowly learnt to trust. Now all the good
help is gone, he feels he can spot liars
with one look; and if he could, he would
take care of her himself. *All these prayers*

for a new body! She doesn't understand
the joke, but simply stares out the window
where an old broken-down tractor stands

in the backyard, grass screaming out of
worn sprockets, joints rusting above slow
gulfs of shadow shot wild with foxglove.

Savannah Chapel

We'd buried our dead knowing women sucked cock
for a loaf of bread or a dirty dollar bill in the city, but here
the barbershop quartet jazzed up songs by Sam Cooke
and Al Green, the onyx sky folding over a thousand acres
of scrubland – evening oils weeping on the flat horizon.
Arm in arm, boaters and Ascot hats, the congregation
took to seats on bales lined as pews – the pearled flair

of expensive perfumes drifting softly over zebra aloe.
Now and then a safari truck dropped off a small party.
Elderly couples, from the trophy lounge, stood partly
lost before being led to chairs – their backs sinking low
into the rounded comfort of velvet sofas made to cradle
the carapace of old age. Bored teenage girls took slow
sure steps to ogle cars that shone like modern miracles,

the clean, bright angles parked where stubborn grass
and bush tomatoes fought disc and harrow to become
a curious parking lot; flat crowns dotted squat across
the golden landscape. Bridesmaids and the groom's
men walked circles, studying the earth in brand-new
shoes they'd never wear again. Restless children threw
tantrums, fenced with sticks – simply testing the sum

of their mothers' patience – who dusted off suits tight
at the seams, spat on thumbs to wipe their children's
faces clean. Then, with a fluidity achieved in dreams,
the reverend raised his hand, the quartet fell to a light
melodious hum, the air thinned and the sky turned pale
to mother-of-pearl. Roosting birds settled from flight,
a dust-driven breeze slithered lazily through the bales.

The congregation settled and straightened their backs.
Sharp-eyed parents admonished children with a glance
before gasps from the back rows fired a collective climax
sparked by the groom and guides riding in on elephants;
behind the groom, a horse-drawn carriage. The spectacle
conjured mixed measures of awe; the closer they got, people
stepped back from their seats. Suspicious of chance,

and ill at ease, others eyed their cars and thumbed their keys;
but most, most were lost to the almighty magnificence
of the beasts. And as though to further pronounce
our disbelief, the ground trembled... At the altar's crease
seven elephants knelt to spontaneous dance and song.
Women rolled ululate tongues. One man rose from his knees
in tears and said, *Perhaps the funeral days are gone.*

And from this utterance, all the joy of love returned
with such wild, unbridled flamboyance. Promised
steps drawing us along, promised hand to promised hand,
a different future fresh and kept from our jaundiced
views. It's true, we'd walked through something dark;
and though the sun set like a weeping wound, the stark
nature of our joy drew us up, and almost embarrassed us.

Mercantile Rain

Before all sorts of retro disco struts or *robot-moves* begin,
before seventies cover songs and empty crates of champagne,
the cake comes in sparkling bright with candles from an age
blessed with every success garnered from this new life.
The colonel stands, lifting his glass. The tent's raised stage
rocked by thunder – earth and sky fast flicked with a knife-
      white light drawing out the long squeal of the microphone...

True perfumes smell like insect repellent in this weather.
An early dinner, long birthday speeches before the thunder
landed its haunting echo, the colonel's loss of words, flute
up in the air like a crystal arum on fire against the pregnant
horizon. Once young and bell-cheeked, proud and resolute,
the colonel said to his wife, *We must leave here after the rains,*
      because the war is coming. And so the war came –

loud with every death, dark with every monstrous fear.
No one survived, except him. Wife and son ambushed near
the border, brother silent since crossing to Mozambique,
mother buried in a bricked-up well; and when the Runde
swells, villagers can still taste the blood, the river's sick
black cream. And he remembers his wife nodding , thunder
      folding over the hut, fields bright with burning cane.

So they dance, the sweet lawn dry beneath the canvas tent,
music and French wine, the whispering rain the bold servant
of old memories. And the cover songs know no family but
the large room he sleeps alone in, troubled by grieving, dead
drunk, lost in the heated valley that floods his heart – the hot
blood of men oiling his grip, the war still ruling his bed,

      wet with squeals carved beneath his brother's cheekbones...

Zvita

Study the bone. The waxed coat stiff with flies.
         Dark corroded holes, missing eyes
sucking light into a cave of teeth, gypsum-white
on black, rigid tongue lost above a lung of steel.
Down the jaw, yellow flume – the slow, slick gel
         of albumin flowing over death's chalice,
down the belly's protruding cavity. A red termite
mound hitches the spine cruelly. The back's awkward
arch parting rigid legs, pushing the pelvis forward
         to give birth to death's black oozing grease.
Labour is drawn; silent as hoof and horn. Stones
bake flat on the valley's hearth. Sinew on bone
lies wet in a slick private darkness, rich suet
         soups warm around muscle till a blanket
of white work carves the skeleton out. Sun and rain
blend perfumes we never trust. The ancient oils
of life, rich with spent secretions, returned to soil –
anointing a seed unfurled through the pelvic crown.

John Eppel

Christmas in Bulawayo

A hallelujah of Heuglin's robins
wakes me from a troubled sleep, troubled not
by regrets or misgivings but by hymns,
hymns of mosquitoes, high-pitched, pin-thin; prick
of crickets, strident cicadas, squirrels
bickering; and the blessing of soft rain
on a tin roof. Smell the frangipanis –
their blossoms, the milk of their bark, rotting
leaves, rotting into humus, life-giving
soil – earthworms, chongololos, flying ants;
and smell that neighbourly ham: pineapple,
cloves; basted with beer and honey: baking.

Expectant pets get meaty bones, rubber
toys, kapenta soaked in leftover soup.
Here comes the postman for his Christmas box,
here the garbage men, ZESA, WATER; queues
and queues of the homeless, the unemployed,
the downtrodden, the hungry and thirsty,
the poor in spirit, the mourners, the meek,
the merciful, the peacemakers, the pure
in heart, the righteous; for theirs is the love
of a Jewish man who was sacrificed
so we may celebrate his birth, and so
we may learn that death makes life beautiful.

Appropriating the Land

We did dams, brown roads with middle-
mannetjies and suppressed
ant hills. We introduced fiddle-
wood for its autumn-stressed
hues and the way its falling petals
sounded like rain. We did
chip geysers, Blair toilets, landfills…
We mapped grid after grid.

We erected bossy warnings
with words like 'forbidden'
and 'only'. We blue-pencilled springs,
used an ancient midden
to support a retaining wall,
re-named *uthsani*. We did
Napier Avenue, Town Hall…
planning grid after grid.

We wrote poems about sunsets,
jacarandas, blue skies,
the dispositions of our pets,
and the fish eagle's cries.
We wrote about bitter longing,
sometimes florid, sometimes terse –
metaphors and symbols thronging,
verse after verse after verse.

Mothy

(in *terza rima*)

The sun declines below its hectic light,
the patient moon is waiting in the wings
as you prepare the agent of the night

to guide me where eternal whisperings
of wasted poets who have gone before,
alert me to the life and death of things.

The moth's desire, with scaled intent, to soar
above the roof tops to a waiting star,
then flutter past its shadow on the core

of this apple, is our desire. Afar
and near, these binaries dissolve like salt
in tears, like sparks in the crepuscular;

time for creatures of this echoing vault
to eat and be eaten, to scuttle, rage,
scuttle and rage; time for us to exalt

in eternal whisperings, engage
in matters of the gut...
but see, the moon has rolled on to the stage;
time, now, for you to sleep, for me to strut.

My Muse

My muse is a woman:

Not one of the nine

No, not Mnemosyne

Not my mother

Not my sister

Not my daughter

Not my lover

Not even you

But my muse is a woman:

The woman in me.

John Eppel

Young Woman Walking

She walks in blue jeans, and the light
is blinking droplets from a slight
gap where sigh and sigh meet the swell,
the swing, of a clapperless bell,
shifting with each stride, diamond bright,
 walking away, winding the spell,

headlong towards a glow-wormed night,
disencumbered tail of a kite
ascending, unbridled, pell-mell
into the labyrinth, smell
of figs beginning to split, tight
blue jeans, phosphoric plasma gel.

Thus I, ageing heteroclite,
pencil in hand, sit down and write.

Too Late

Sad words,

the saddest some say.

Now you will go your way

while I resume, like stirred dregs in a tea cup,

a slow sinking...

slowly sinking.

It's only when he lost it

that Adam longed for Eden;

only when she died

that Emma became much missed by her poet;

only when another shocked you into beauty

that I, like dust on a still day,

resumed a slow sinking...

slowly sinking.

John Eppel

When Will Men Learn

When will men learn to grow old
like their bodies –
gout in the big toe,
crystals in the knee,
ruptured groin,
cracked rib,
neck spasms,
skin cancer,
dry eyes,
deaf ears...
only the nose – lingering humid thrill –
so that the ache of loss may,
with every distancing glass of wine,
resolve itself into a pretzel?

Game of 12 Moons

«*Déjà de traits en l'air s'élevait un nuage;*
Déjà coulait le sang, prémices du carnage.»
Racine, *Iphigénie*

"*My dear nephew, I must tell you*
of your father's death
we all hope you'll be able to attend
the forty-days' wake."
Ahmed Tidjani-Cisse, 'Home News'

I

We set down our arms and waited. The sky turning black. Fatigue haunting us

When he looked into her eyes
he knew the world would not
change greatly after his death.
Her skin, warm – olive brown,

her fingers playing a delicate
melody on his knurled spine –
her breath sweet with the tune
of the rain spilling off her lips.

His tears fell silently. Sparkled.
Moonlight glistened off grass.
This is how our deepest miseries
are made to shine, he thought.

II

The Season Changed

with the drum of boots through each village.
The dead marched out in uniformed splinters
through the silence of men's dreams, men
who feared the worst of what was to come.

Through fields, over hills, the dead marched –
their children born to bear terrible histories,
the murderous banner of the sun tattooed to
tongues savouring the sweet taste of blood.

III

Where the Dead Fold their Sweet Limbs

is where hearts of youths were lost
deep in the damp ditches of forests
where trees guard the windless
dark. The dead lie in each other's
arms, shallow fires in hollow skulls,
the wind circling, howling in haunts
where troubled whispers dissolve.

IV

The sun bowed its head and weighed the fate of its kingdom

Why they could not wait for him to die
was as clear and simple as anything could be.
He looked aged, ravaged by life, jaundiced;
the carefree glimmer in his eyes had faded.

They'd been waiting for this all their lives.
Beneath the austere ministry of his gaze
a terrible cell began to sprout – What joy!
they felt, all waiting with baited breaths.

V

Patrice shut himself out from the world and forbade his servants to read aloud

Yes, some things were left, she wasn't purely gone.
He felt this when the candlelight began to falter
after each dose of gin. Listening to the last track
on the album, he remembered simple things: how
they first met, her only wanting to fuck in the dark,
her obsession with cardamom. They were too young
to say they'd stick it out till the end, the end ending
with no children. And now – the phone's sexiness
fails the promise, his last gin done – the needle
skipping repeatedly over the last track of the album.

VI

The Great Cause of the Platinum Tribe

He failed to see how he had not been strong.
To him, she was merely a woman. Her arms
merely women's arms. Strange, he could
not think of anything but her, and felt the
sad weight of guilt build upon his weakness.

VII

An apparition of soldiers disappears into the mist

As a child she feared puppets,
puppets of any sort,
even after the animate lives
were demystified by a show of hands –
it was still too much to bear.
Even now, when she closes her eyes,
she sees their lifeless limbs –
her parents' awkward gaze
gauzed black with flies.

VIII

A pot of ink on a table where a gramophone plays music during the war

She arrived late, wearing a pearl necklace
around her wrist, knee-high boots,
a long coat and black beret.

He sat in the bar drinking whiskey and soda,
pretending to read the evening's
programme.

IX

He stared deep into the eyes of the man he was about to kill. Sweat fell from his brow.
The sky pregnant with rain

She had been playing the game

with her shadow,

the game of twelve moons –

lifting floorboards in the kitchen,

whispering hurriedly to herself.

The sun would rise soon,

the smell of the air would change,

as would everything else

in the forest.

X

Graf vom Strahl appears to Käthchen in an angelic vision

All he could do when he woke
was smell her hair.
In her hair – the smell of others would come.
He could say nothing,
this world was not theirs.
The water he had left in the bucket
the night before sat flat and unused.
As the sun rose, he washed his face,
placed the bucket
beside the door.
Watched her sleep.
And felt dirty.

XI

Negotiations in a room with the world looking on

His clothes stuck to his skin, damp with sweat.
His reading glasses steamed up when he stepped out
of the air-conditioned car. He felt reassured when
he noticed the other man was missing a leg
and wore a dated uniform.

He missed Elise, his mood coloured by her absence.
Flies and heat bothered him. Cameras flashed.
Two nights before this – his mother had died;
he had nearly given her Christianity.

XII

Che pensieri soavi, che speranze!

What great friends they had become.

A few years before he had marched through villages

aching to be known – young, and full of ambition;

now they sat together, over a beer and dinner,

playing chess, building bridges of war.

XIII

The bloodshed had begun in the dreams of many faraway

Urban hedgerows made him anxious,
yet the hawk moths fascinated him.
Every evening, after sunset, he'd watch
the creatures skim and dart from petal
 to petal, the pallid sky yawning,
the wild studded darkness closing in.

XIV

The door flew open. Men rushed in screaming, shooting

The dreams are unrelenting:
she allows his dark weight to sink
deep into her, the musk of sweat
roaring into her nostrils – hot over
her neck. No amount of touching
could kill his desire. In the early
hours of the morning she moans.
Masturbating hard like a teenager.

XV

They began hanging carpenters and priests

Asphyxiating humidity. 103°F shade:
the only refuge for flies. Something
lay rotting amid trunks of silent trees.
The earth black with a buzz weaving
its heavy noise over the hidden stench.

Everything casual. Until a forearm
locked tight around his throat. There
was no time to fight back. He choked
staring at the moon hanging pale
in the sky – the sky blue and beautiful.

XVI

The days grew shorter, the nights colder by the hour

He could not remember the old town,
yet this image persistently recurred:
a driveway wild with bougainvillea,
two golden Labradors asleep
by the fender of a car propped up on bricks.
Beside the car pungent sunlight fell
hard on a bleached doll's head,
the featureless face staring up to the sky,
the bald head cradled on a crate
of empty beer bottles.

XVII

Q

Candlelight. Honeydew honey.
Lemon and whiskey. Shadows
and the sound of rain. Shortwave
frequencies sketch a dark theatre
on dirty walls. A hoarse throat,
a dream of swooping raptors
spraying talons over compost –
apes and birds, the wet noise of
fever making art of weakened
cries, his cries drawn and dry.

XVIII

What would become of the widows' daughters

And he let his mind roam the landscape

others had always owned on their breath –

the beauty of mist and light, the grandeur of silence.

On the sofa the two of them cuddled,

warm and snug – wine in their heads.

A song turned in his heart, sweet with poetry,

their love true. The sun had set.

The moon rising blood red

over hills where both their mothers were born.

XIX

His brother had held his hand at his father's funeral. This was the last time he'd see his brother, or his brother's family again

i

It was agreed. Imported cherry wood.

The in-laws enjoyed this new history,

corporate art hanging on the walls, loud

and expensive. Marble floors, Catholic

sculptures polished white with treaties

scored with the coo of doves on glass –

histories of vines sweeter than any nectar,

cellars packed to the rafters with grief.

Do you know you scream in your dreams?

A stranger's name curdles deep in her throat –

her hands reaching out, scrambling at

the ceiling – the ceiling red with stars.

ii

and if you are fluent in bloodletting

this unanswered war becomes elegant

in the mind's sweat-blurred terrain

where language is more than love or sorrow

where faces peel back to reveal the bone

of time

iii

So let them bond the way they wish,

and bite each other's tongues

to taste the blood and seal their fate.

Let the sky anoint wounds

with something simpler than prayer,

let the bond of war bleed into love,

and the blood of our language reign.

Epilogue

Caminantes, no hay caminos. Hay que caminar

Without the salts beneath his nose,
the land had not changed, the smoke
and constant wailing had grown even more tiresome.
There was laughter too – a sort of strained laughter
contorted by the grip of hunger and sorrow.
With every birth, love wept like a wound
refusing to heal, the sky dazed and indifferent
with a blind sun rising reluctantly and setting fast.
The music of the world became industrial,
his spirit huddling in his heart, eyes closed,
unwilling to ever venture out
        into what was now all lost.

Printed in April 2018
by Gauvin Press,
Gatineau, Québec